Big Sailor

My First Big ABC

Ages 3-5

Vol.1 A·B·C

Paprikadu!
Your study buddy

My First Big ABC Book Series
Big Sailor Edu

Copyright © 2021 Cambridge Dynasty Press

For permission requests, bulk order information, or any business related inquries, please contact the publisher at the email address below.

Cambridge Dynasty Press
30 N Gould St. STE4000
Sheridan, WY 82801
Email: Bestsailoredu@Gmail.com

Written, Designed, and Printed in the United States of America

978-1-7357844-3-4(Paperback)

47678459

Hi! Nice to meet you. My name is Paprikadu!

I am your study buddy for this book!

1. Building Skills for Pen Control
2. Recognizing Alphabet Letters
3. Building Confidence
4. Enjoying a Good Book
5. Being Patient with Practice
6. Developing Creative Thinking
7. Being Proud of Achievement
8. Having Fun

This book belongs to

_____
(name)

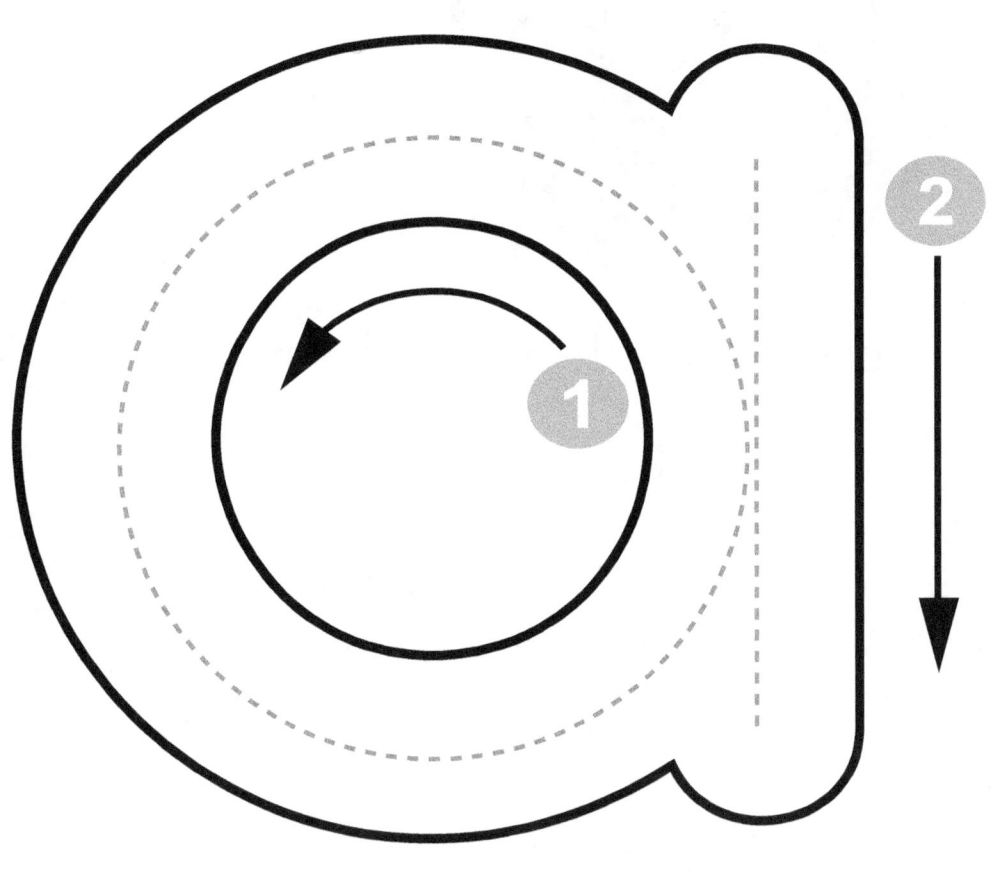

 Read out loud

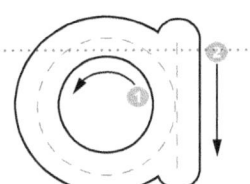 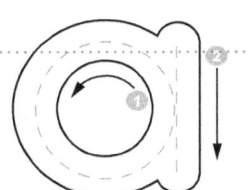 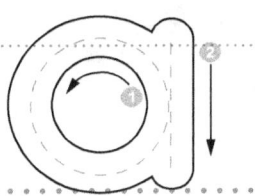 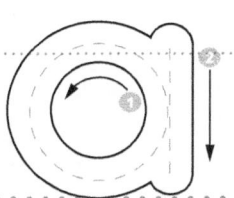

Apple

 Let's trace following the numbers

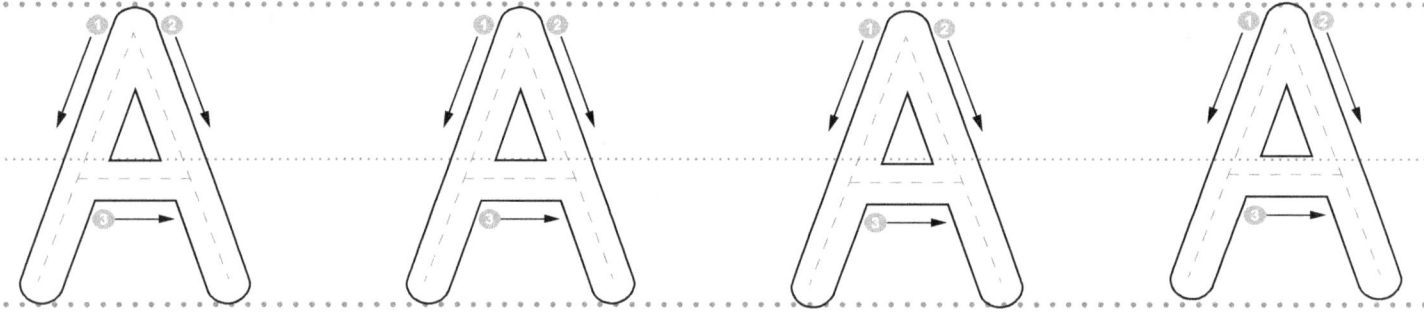

Airplane

 ant

 Read out loud

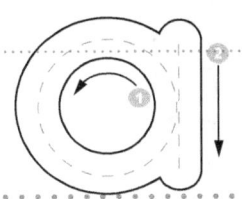 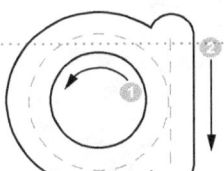 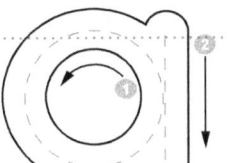 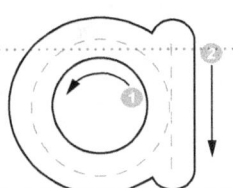

 alligator

Find every A and color them

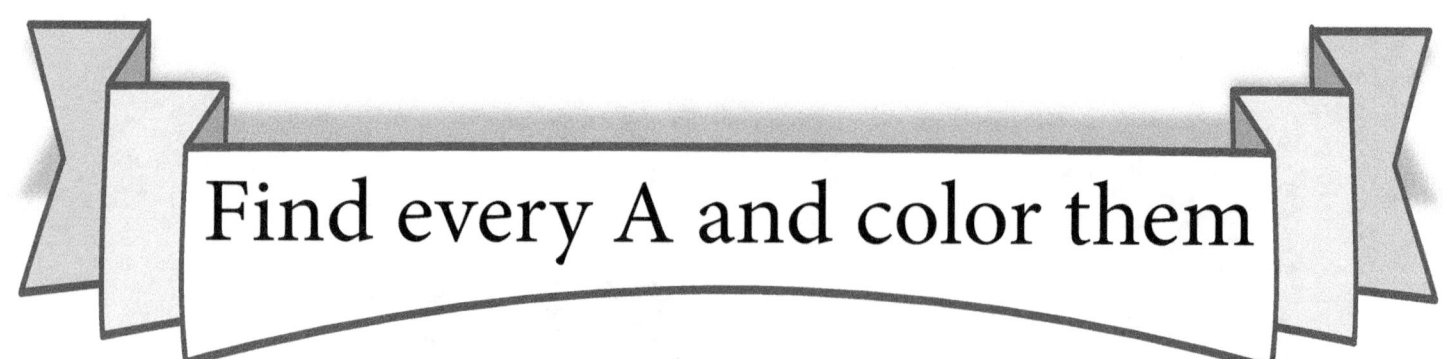

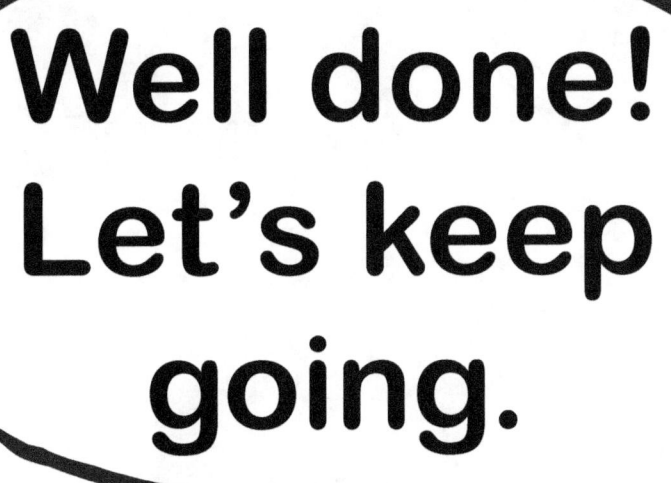

Trace the dotted line and read out loud

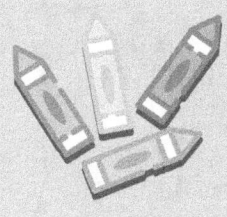 # Find every A and color the sections

Find every a and circle them

a for ant

Trace the dotted line and read out loud

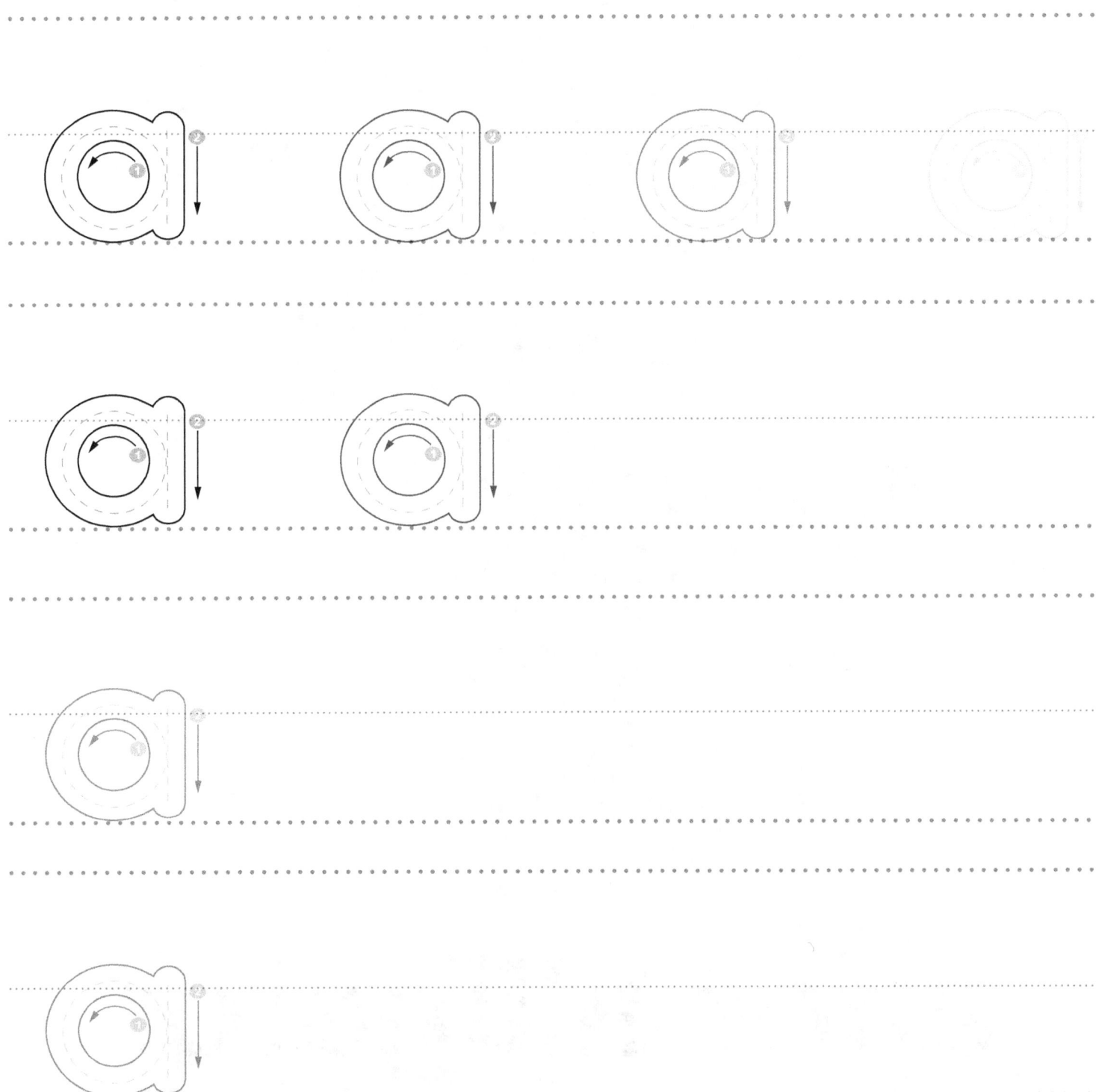

15

a for alligator

Draw lines to match

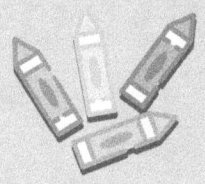 **Find every a and color the sections**

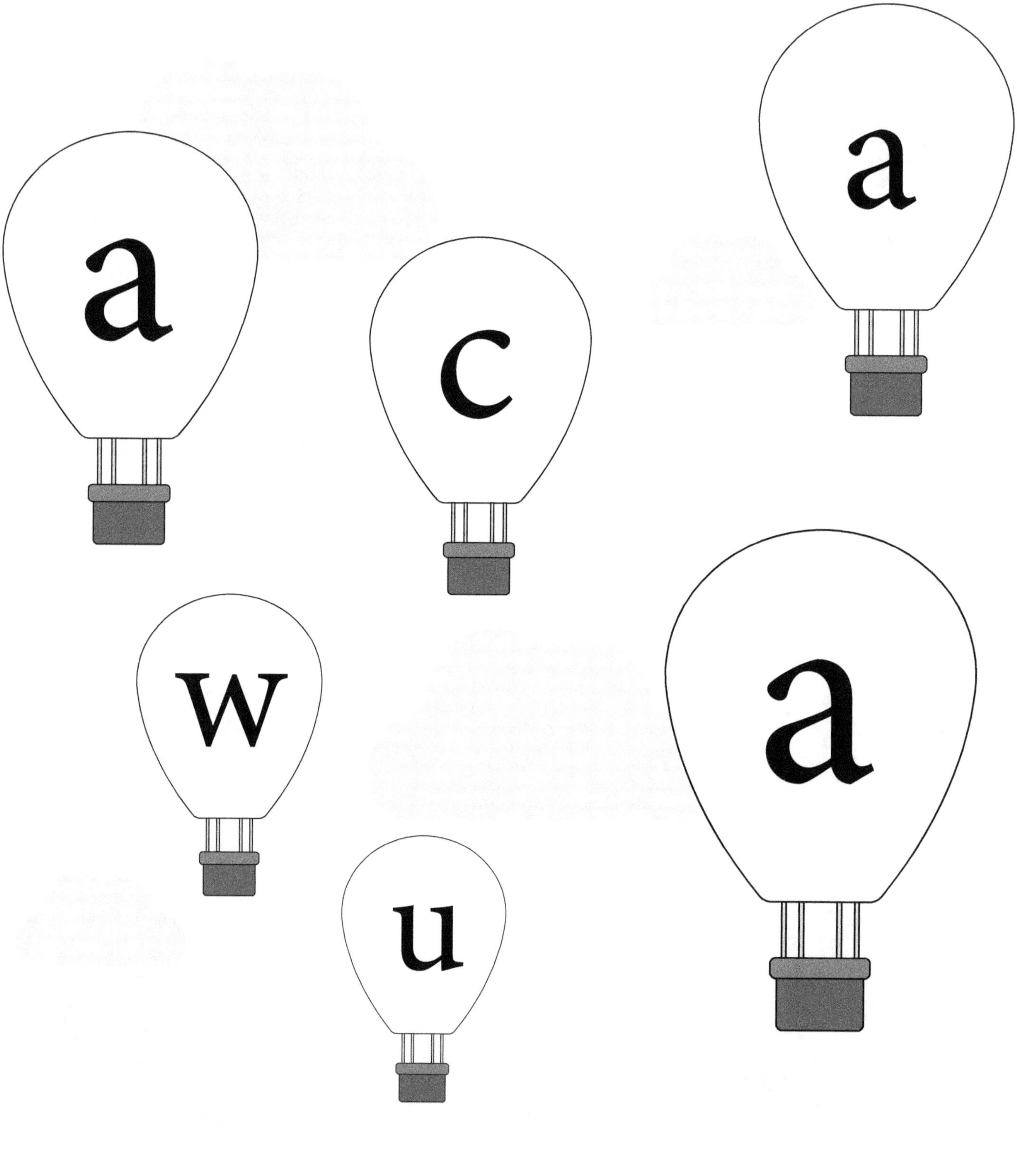

Trace the dotted line and read out loud

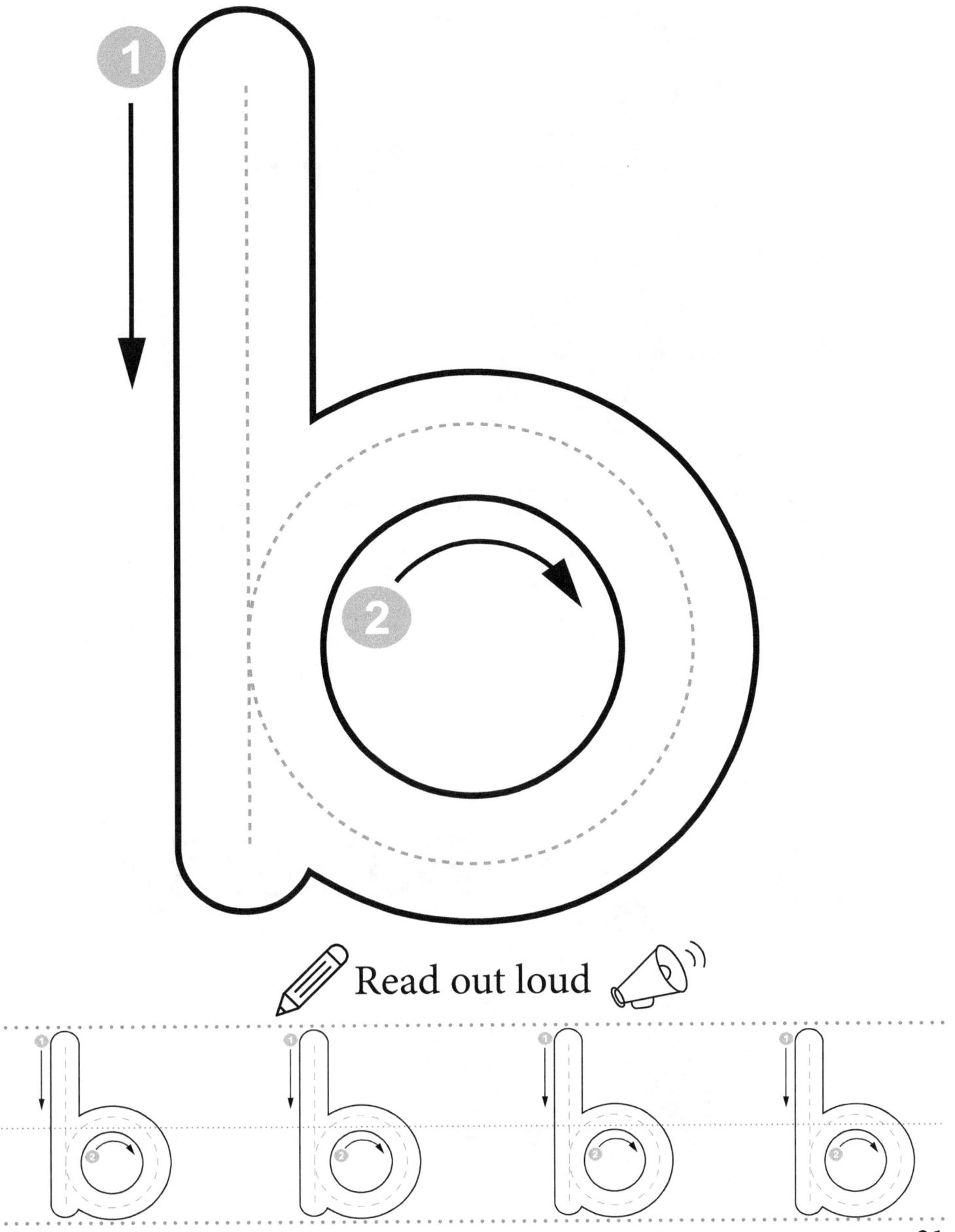

Bird

✏️ Let's trace following the numbers 📢

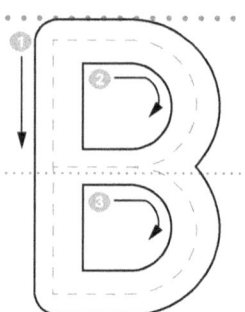 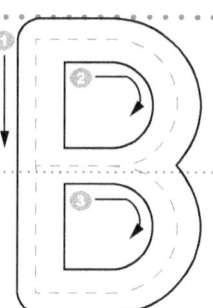 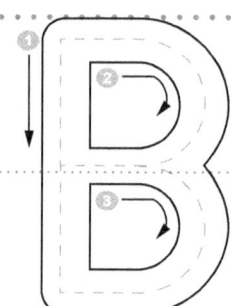 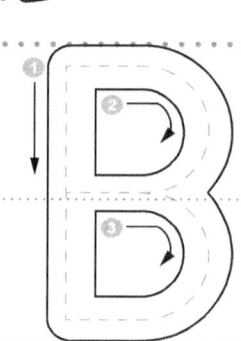

Butterfly

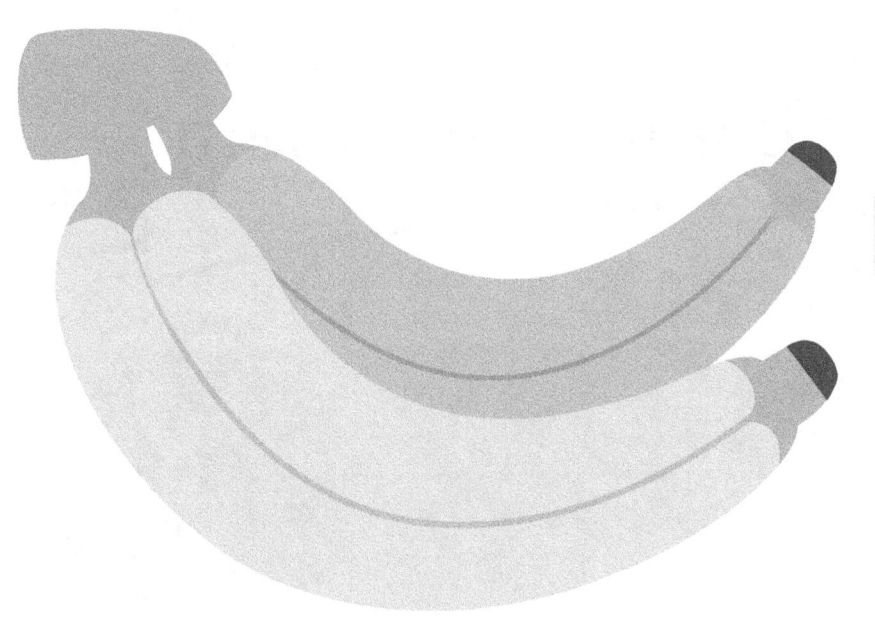

banana

🖉 Read out loud 📣

b b b b

bee

Find every B and color them

Trace the dotted line and read out loud

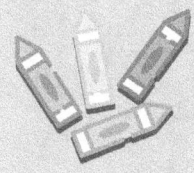 # Find every B and color the sections

Paprikadu

Find every b and circle them

b for bird

Trace the dotted line and read out loud

Draw lines to match

b for bee

 # Find every b and color the sections

Trace the dotted line and read out loud

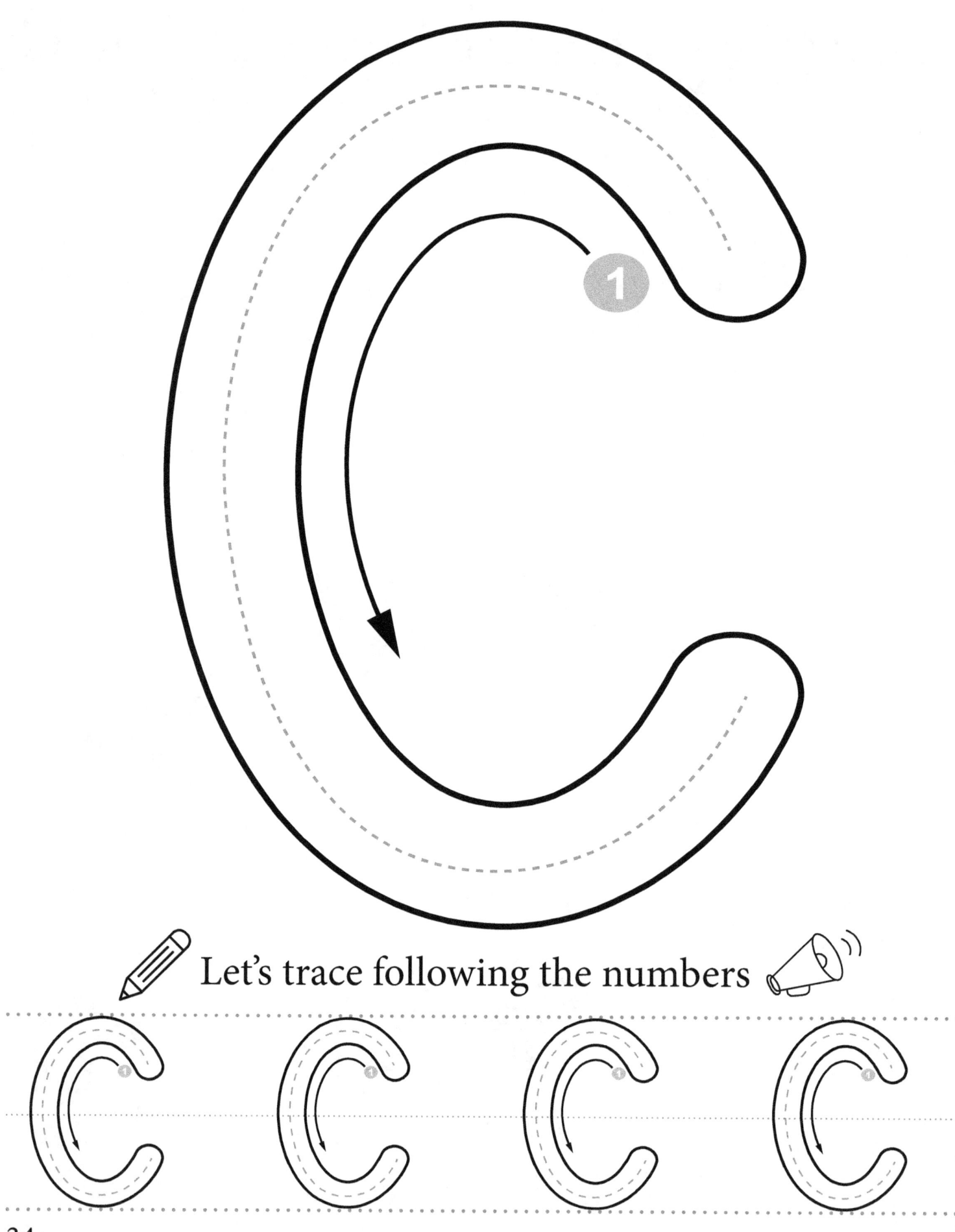

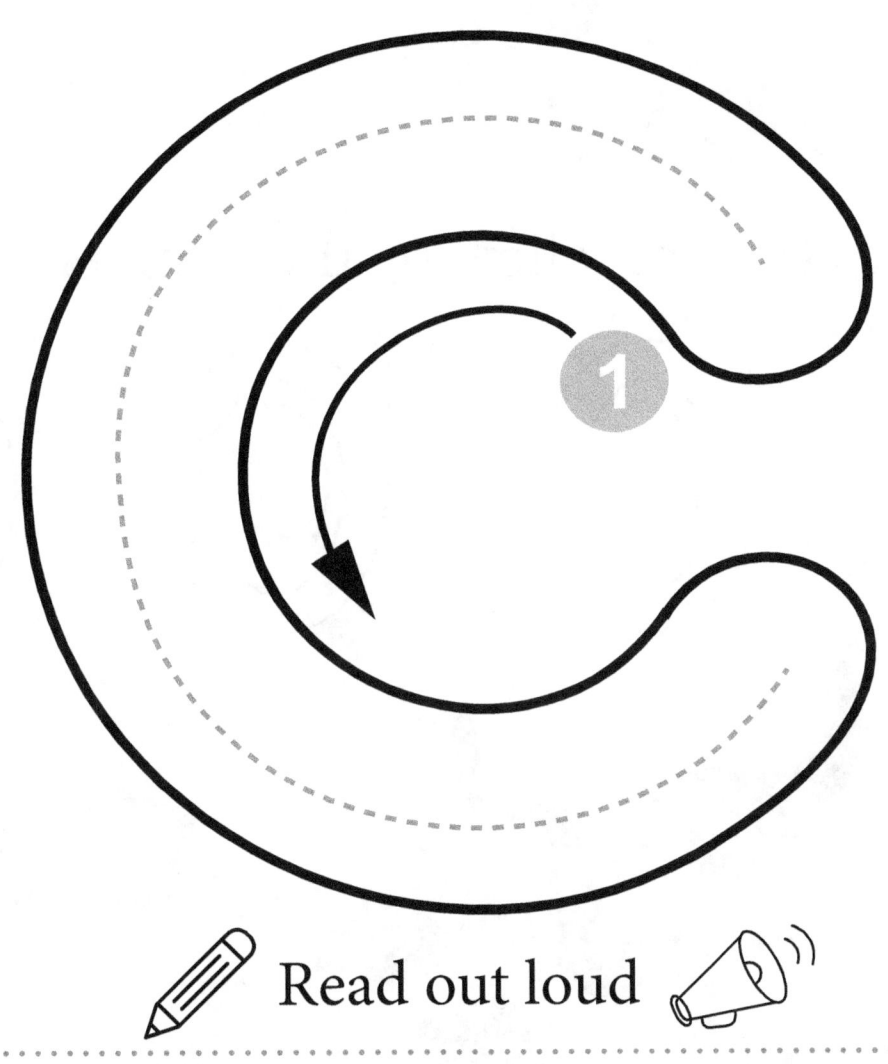

✏️ Read out loud 📢

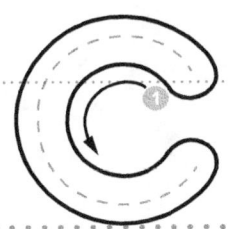 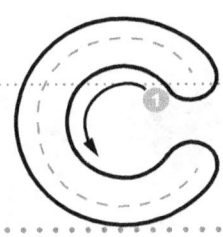 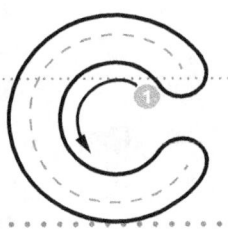 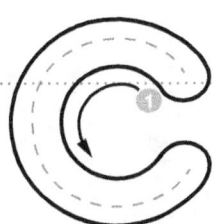

Cake

 Let's trace following the numbers

C C C C

Cow

cat

 Read out loud

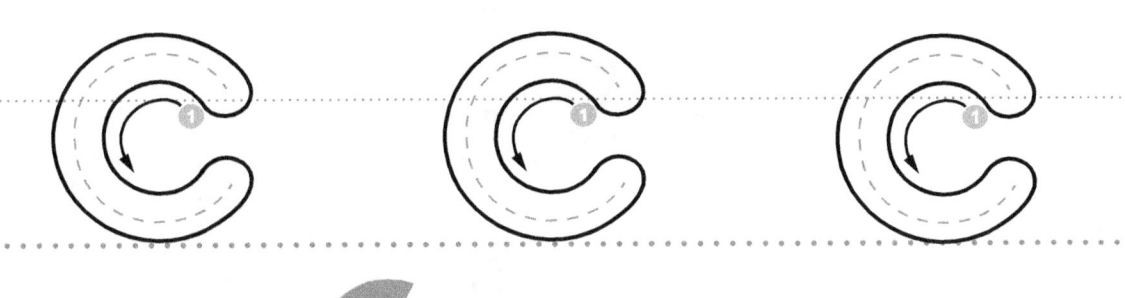

crab

Find every C and color them

Trace the dotted line and read out loud

 # Find every C and color the sections

Paprikadu

Find every c and circle them

c for cat

Trace the dotted line and read out loud

c for cupcake

Draw lines to match

 **Find every c and color the sections**

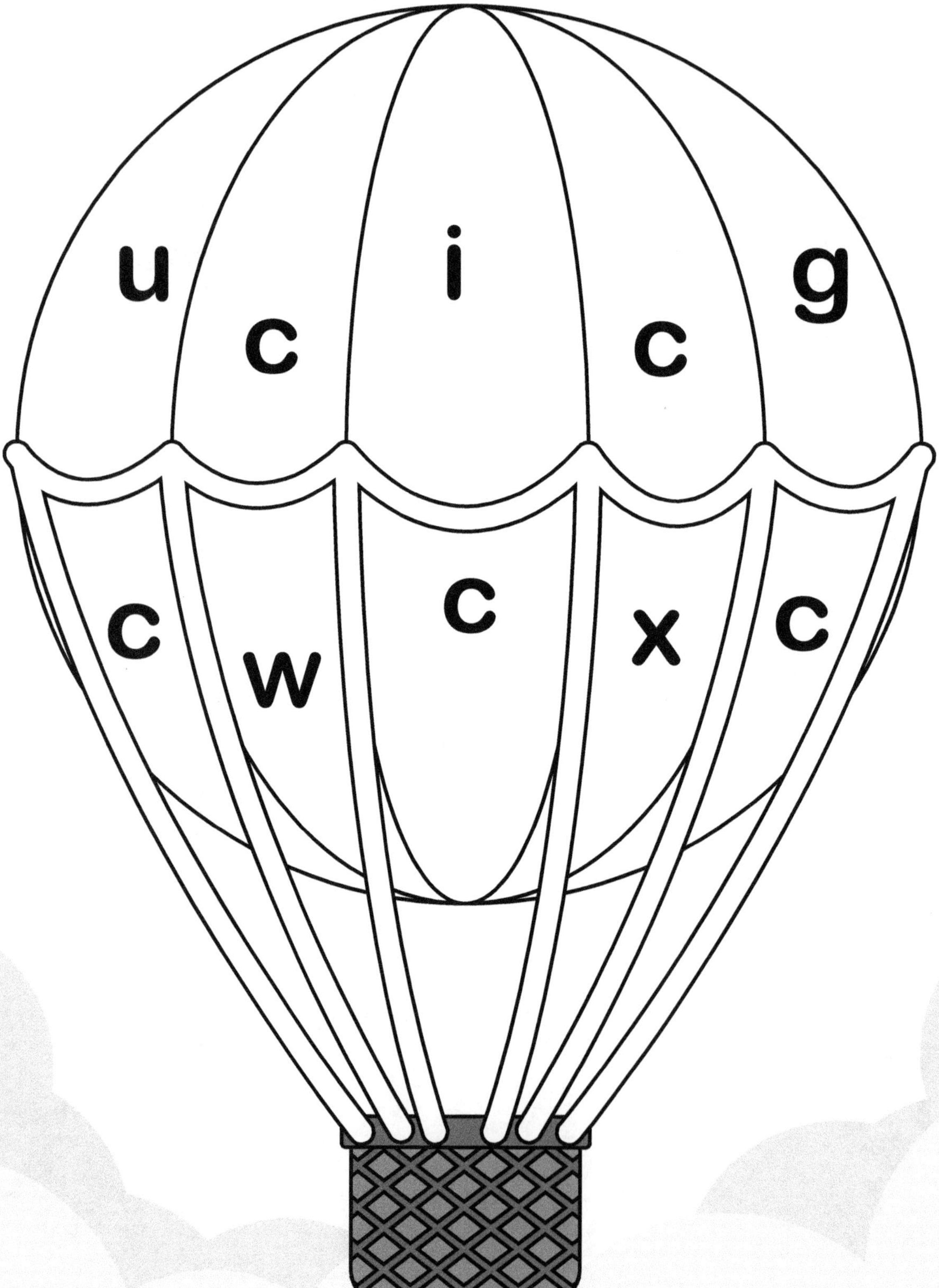

Trace the dotted line and read out loud

Where is Paprikadu?

Find and circle!

Let's express your

I am cool

I am hungry

I am playful

I am proud

I am okay

feelings with Paprikadu!

 # Let's express your

I am sad

I am calm

I am rushing

I am frustrated   I am angry

feelings with Paprikadu!

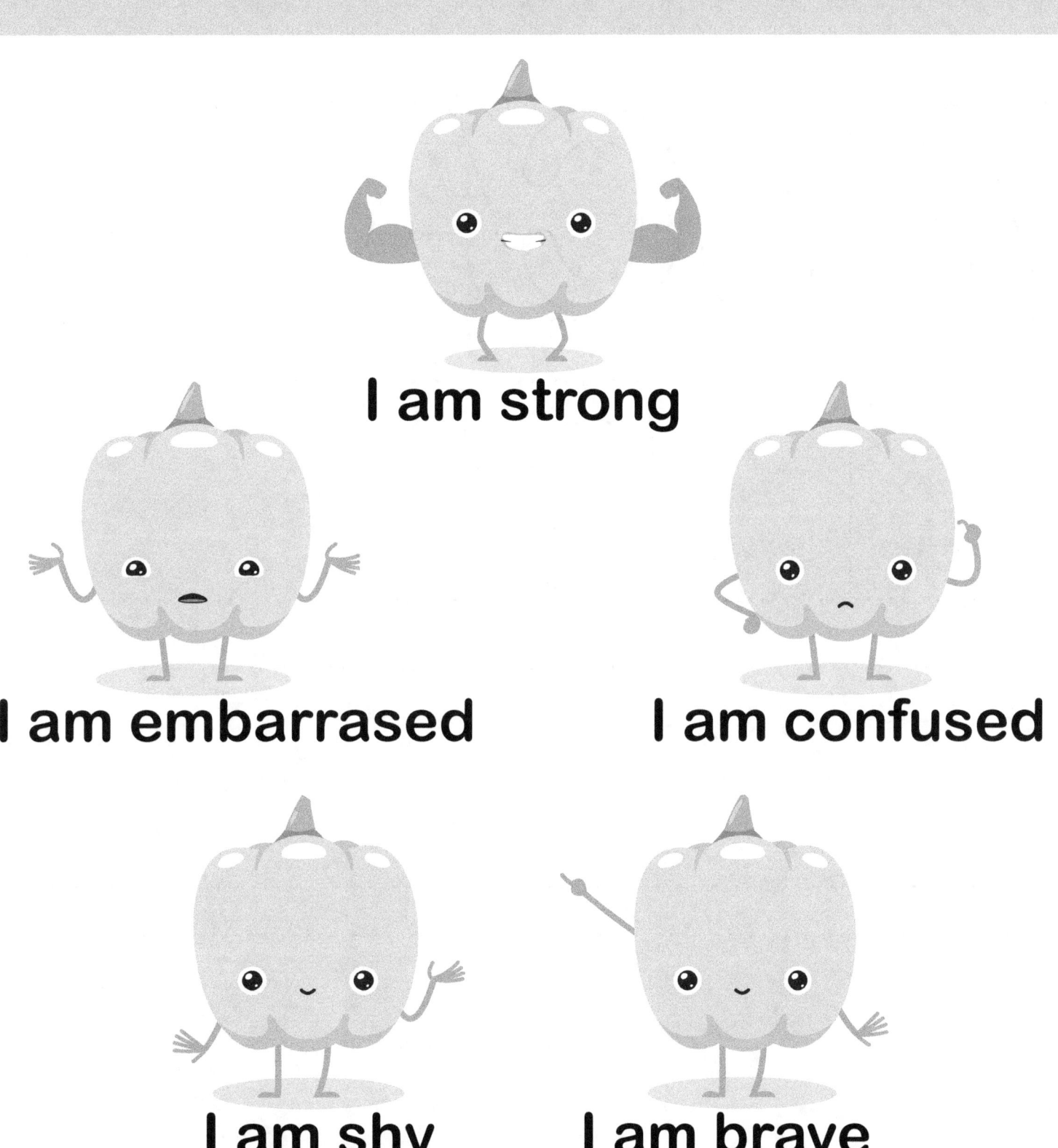

I am strong

I am embarrased I am confused

I am shy I am brave

Write ABC and read out loud

ABCABC

ABC

ABC

ABC

Write abc and read out loud

abc abc

abc

abc

abc

Award

You are amazing!

This award is for

_____ _____
(first name)   (last name)

Great job finishing the book!

Date: _____

Visit Our Website

BigSailorEdu.com

and Get Free & Fun

Educational Material

ABC Workbook Series by Big Sailor Edu

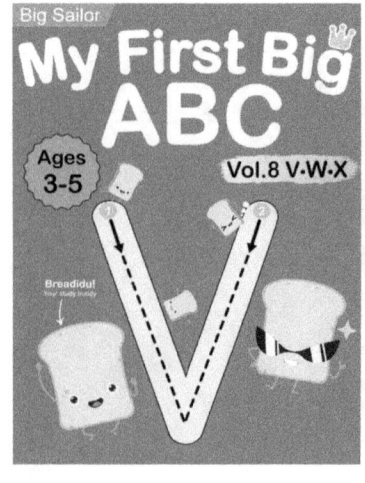

Cambridge Dynasty Press

www.ingramcontent.com/pod-product-compliance
Lightning Source LLC
Chambersburg PA
CBHW081421080526
44589CB00016B/2626